JEHOVAH FASHIONISTA
(So Fashionistic!)

**God's got Stunning & Amazing
Fashion Statement
Check it out!**

Fodeke
Adunni Opeoluwa

JEHOVAH Fashionista

God's Got Stunning and Amazing Fashion Statement
Check it out...!

For Further Enquiries, Please contact

Phone no: **07041975383**, 08077737347
Email: opeoluwa@pecrevelations.org.ng
Facebook: @pecrevelations
Youtube: Fashion Smart Christians Tv
Instagram: @adunniopeoluwa

No portion of this publication may be reproduced without prior permission, reprinted or transferred without prior permission of the author.

Address: 7 Tako 1 Road, Tako – Ajara, Badagry, Lagos.
Office Address: Alafia House, Plot 8 Block 2, Ogun State Housing Corp. Residential Estate, Sango Ota, Beside Mobil Petrol Station, Ogun State
First Edition: November, 2020

Preface

God has a great sense of beauty and more fascinating is the discovery that he's got a high taste for fashion and style? This book seeks to reveal God's Profile in the expertise of Dress Making and Fashion Designing. From biblical accounts, we see this chronicling from making of simple coats to the prowess and dexterity God displayed in the exquisite designing of a very elegant and flamboyant dress code. This was as demonstrated, in a whole chapter where the intricacies which went into the dress God designed was vividly spelt out in the directives He gave to Moses. And, as recorded in some portions of the scripture, the rare artistic skills and touch of elegance displayed by him is second to none!

This discovery of God's fashion statement, gradually moves to a crescendo when we saw him recount how he demonstrated and gave a vivid account of his expertise as he dressed up a daughter of his, with his touch of radiance, beauty and splendor! You want to know more? Just go check out and discover this amazing side of God which promises to be both entertaining and equally inspiring. This helps us to learn how to savour some of the various beauty concepts which the Lord has created and equally took time out to model for us. The Essence which has to do with leading us on how best to get necessary benefits derivable from beauty and fashion aspects of life, for a pleasurable experience and spiritual empowerment towards enlargement of His coast and Kingdom here on earth, to His glory and praise.

What's more? If you are a Beauty and Fashion Expert or Enthusiasts, this book is a must-read. It will make you discover the fashion side of God, giving you a better standing and a broader perspective regarding demands of your profession as a tailor or fashion designer set out to excel, as well seeking to be peculiar, distinct and different, against all odds in accordance with the expectations of the one I fondly call the Author of Fashion. I mean the one the bible calls the Author and Finisher of our Faith. And if you are not a fashion designer, but simply passionate about looking good and beautiful, if you are just a fashion lover, reading this book would help you become more confident about asserting yourself and authenticating who you are as one representing His kingdom here, who should be attractive at all times. As a Leader, a Minister of the word, spiritual guide and a pastor in mission, this book comes handy as a veritable resource for reference, thereby making ministering a lot easier, particularly when speakers find themselves on this very important aspect and versatile page of life, called beauty, fashion, life and style. A page and a phase we can neither overlook nor undermine in our walk with God and our work in the building up of His body. As we dig deeper into his word on this all-important area of ministry, together, we can play our individual and unique role in the entire scope of God's agenda for humankind via vis-à-vis Beauty, Fashion, Life and Style.

DEDICATION
A BEAUTIFUL POEM TO THE GOD OF BEAUTY

Precious Father, I dedicate this book to you as the one who I fondly call the ultimate Fashionista, the Author of every good thing called fashion. The one whose Exquisite Fashion Statement as recorded, is second to none! My very own "Jehovah ATTRACTIVE", you were so attractive to me, so much that I could not resist getting attracted and drawn to you over 3 decades ago. Illuminated by your word, when my inner eyes became eventually open to the wondrous beauty in your person and personality. Your kind of Beauty, which is light and illuminating, dispelling the ugliness of darkness around me, little wonder I immediately got magnetized towards you. This was in response to your kind love, grace, mercy and tender care which you graciously extended towards me to date. And trust me Father, I'm loving it! I mean, your attractiveness and your ageless beauty. How sweet! How wonderful! How Sincere! How pure!

You are the God I fondly call the veritable author of Beauty, the author of Fashion, the author of Life and Style, the veritable author of all good and lovely things. Yes! the Author and the Finisher of our Faith; and this faith, comprising of every good thing that has to do with us, your children. I worship you Lord with everything you blessed me with, which enable me to be beautiful, look beautiful, fashionable, lively and stylish to the glory of your name alone. Therefore, once again, precious Lord, I declare with a heart of deep worship, that I dedicate this book to the one person, whom I call "BEAUTY PERSONIFIED", the one whose BEAUTY IS NOT JUST PERFECT but is truly BEAUTIFUL and PURE INSIDE OUT! Lord, you are the only one whose incorruptible and ageless beauty can never fade away! Precious Father, you are the one some refer to as ROSE OF SHARON, THE LILY OF THE VALLEY. And to crown it, according to your words, I attest to the fact that, truly you are THE KING OF GREAT BEAUT-KING OF GLORY! Glorious and Gracious Lord, please receive this token of my honour and adoration to you, for you are not just ADORABLE, you are ABLE, CAPABLE and more than worthy to receive it!

And now, I round off this special poem by dedicating this book to the one whose name is MAGNIFICIENT and OMNISCIENT, the God who knows all things. The one who graciously reposed the confidence in me, having endowed me with the requisite knowledge to put together this write-up to bless my generation, in order that we, that is, my generation and I, could be effectively poised to make maximal use of beauty, fashion, life and style concepts, as ready and available God-given instruments of praise in our world, for the purpose of deriving as much benefits as possible and above all, to the lifting up of your glorious name. Father, please permit me, and with a heart of humility, to officially crown you, as my King and my one and only Jehovah Attractive and Jehovah Beautiful!

ACKNOWLEDGEMENT

I give all praise and glory to the Maker of all things, the one who made the inspiration, the writing and the publishing of this book possible. I adore the one who gave me the grace to bring out this book, being my fourth book within the space of 8 years, to bless my generation; blessed be your most holy name, oh Lord. **FATHER, I GIVE YOU ALL THE GLORY**!

I equally appreciate my mother, who recently turned 80 years for being a great blessing to me in the journey of my writing and publishing every step of the journey. My dear mother, Elder (Mrs) Mopelola Abike Agboola JP, no doubt God created you and made you to be my Mother for a time like this. Though, times were, when it looked like there would be no support coming from nowhere, God always stepped in, in most remarkable way through you, and a few others. I therefore pray that God will yet make you fulfill purpose before He calls you home and may you see Jesus holding you by the hand, leading you to the Presence of the Father before you see death! Of course, this will happen after you have spent many more years with us, your children and grandchildren, both biological, adopted and spiritual, spread all over the world. Once again, I say **GOD BLESS YOU MOTHER!**

I register my gratitude also to my friend and sister who has been of much inspiration to me, Sister Sarkis Ebunoluwa. I pray that the Lord would continue to count you worthy to carry His flag higher and may you not lose your reward.

To, Mr Sanmi Akindipe, my coach, thanks sir.

My appreciation also goes to members of the Peculiar Revelations Broadcast family, (an umbrella body for (Honouring God Through Dressing Initiative), for your moral support as well as other things you do to lift up this vision, I say, God bless you all.

Lastly, I appreciate every other person that could not be captured right away, whose efforts have contributed immensely towards the success story of this book. To them I say, the good Lord will reward your labour of love.

Content in Chapters

Chapter 1
CHECKING OUT GOD'S DRESS SENSE AND FASHION STATEMENT!

Are you aware that the God we serve has many sides? Have you taken time to discover the Entertainment, Fashion, Style, Artistic and Beauty side of God? **As a Christian Beauty enthusiast and Fashion lover, did you know that God's Fashion Sense is Amazingly Beautiful, Attractive, Gorgeous, Dazzling, Unique, Majestic and so Impressive?**

In fact, for me, one of the reasons I love and admire the God we serve, particularly the God of the Christian Faith is, He portrays himself as an interesting person to be with. Even in fashion life, our God is not some boring and dry fashion person or deity. If you are in doubt, please go check out one of God's Fashion Design Notepads in such books of the bible as, Exodus. It is interesting to note that the whole of chapter 28, comprising 43 verses is dedicated to exquisite designing of a garment. Here we see God manifest himself as a fashion conscious person, when he gave a dress-making directives to Moses. And this is one of the reasons someone like me find Christianity - a Lifestyle so interesting and amazing, the challenges that come with the Christian race, notwithstanding.

By way of background account, the genesis of Cloth wearing actually began in the book of Genesis chapter 3. There, we saw how the Lord made appropriate clothing for Mr and Mrs Adam. This he had to do, when he discovered they were not properly clothed with the type of dress they hurriedly sewed for themselves. This did not cover their bodies well enough. As we progress in biblical account of what I call God's profile in the business of dress making and fashion designing, in Exodus 28, there, we see how God revealed himself, for the first time as an Exquisite Fashion Designer. Here, the Lord, premiered this unique and rare fad. The very cloth being designed, was not just special, it was customized, expensive and a flamboyant one at that! Lovely was the general outlook.

Furthermore, in order to show how God does place much premium on good looks, after instructing Moses on what the design of the customized garment should look like, he directed that he (Moses) ensured expert tailors handled the sewing. In addition, these skilled tailors must possess the wisdom of God needed to handle the special task. And guess, who was to wear this cloth? Aaron, the Priest and his children, who have been assigned the duty of assisting their father with altar affairs. These were the privileged ones to wear the special type of cloth which the God Almighty Himself designed. What a rare honour!

Interestingly, it was this very discovery that made me realize, and pleasantly so, that the God we serve has a good fashion sense, a high taste at that! Again, this is one of the reasons someone like me find Christianity as a Lifestyle, so interesting and fun-filled, not just in clothing affairs, but in some other spheres of life. With regard to this opinion of mine, if I may give some form of advice, I would like to share the line of thought below.

Here, I find relevant and borrowing from a local parlance in Nigeria, God asked me to inform his dear children that, life does not have to be about being ' 'Jim, Jim, all the time. Meaning, one does not have to be uptight every time, appearing unnecessarily serious and overtly sanctimonious even in one's looks. Life does not have to be hard and boring and monotonous all the way, all in the name trying to look sober and religious.

To all God's sweethearts reading this write-up, the Lord says, once in a while, just RELAX and take time out to enjoy this other God-given side of life, manifesting for instance, through Beauty and Fashion. What's more, it is important to state that, the Lord created all these entertainment-related concepts and took time out to MODEL for us, on how to savour a pleasurable experience from them as well. Friends, this is part of what makes this Transient Life more enjoyable and equally less stressful.

Regardless of individual responses to life, one major purpose the Lord led me to put together this write up and share with my generation who are children of God is, once in a while or as deemed fit, it is not out of place to take some time out to RELAX and enjoy life within the confines of the Christian culture and our kingdom Cultural heritage. What's more? One of the ways we could savour this relaxation is to discover what I call the Entertainment side of God. This could manifest in Fashion, Beauty and Style experiences, as we interact and derive our inspiration from our heavenly father, the one who, those of us who are beauty and fashion lovers fondly call the "ROSE OF SHARON and LILLY of the valley. The account of Queen Esther's story readily comes to mind here. She took part in a royal beauty contest and guess what? She got the crown! Not just the crown; she got the highly exalted position as the queen in the Persian Empire. Yes! She became the first lady. And do we know the secret of her success? Please come along.

Chapter 2
PLEASE MAKE WELCOME-JEHOVAH ATTRACTIVE !

As a summary specialist, through the scriptures, what I have come to discover is, the Summary of God's own Fashion Statement can simply be termed – ATTRACTIVE! Mind you, for the purpose of this conversation, when we say "attractive", we refer to what an e.dictionary defines as: Captivating, Beautiful, Stunning, Good-looking, Nice, Lovely, Charming, Charismatic, Appealing and Delightful. So, for me, this is the reason I fondly say, one of Gods' middle names is Jehovah ATTRACTIVE! He is, putting it in the contemporary sense, Jehovah Fashionista.

And for you, you may choose to call him Jehovah Beautiful! Just like the bible reveals some of God's names as Jehovah Shalom – Lord Our Peace, Jehovah Jireh – Lord our Provider, when the Lord reveals Himself to you, as a God who says, He is beautiful for all situations, when He makes all things beautiful in His time, at the set time for your own lifting, particularly when He makes you beautiful by blessing your life with beautiful things, then, friend, you cannot but burst out in joy of adoration and praise to him, thereby responding to Him as either, your dear Jehovah ATTRACTIVE or Jehovah BEAUTIFUL! This, of course depends on the circumstances under which (how) he reveals himself to you. Actually, it was in this manner that, some of those names having the term "Jehovah" as their root word, came about also.

Why call him, Jehovah beautiful? Aside from the fact that in many verses of the scriptures, our God is severally referred to as, the King of Glory. (and the dictionary makes us understand that one of the meanings of the word "glory" is **GREAT BEAUTY**, the book of Psalm also has this to say about Him. "....**out of Zion, God shines forth, Perfect in Beauty!**". Furthermore, "**The ROSE of Sharon** and Lilly of the Valley" is another biblical expression which many use to adore their Lord. Friend, through all these situations, we can connect and experience a completely new dimension and interesting side of God, in the concept called beauty, a side of life whereby we could savour and enjoy an experience filled with fun and great pleasure which, at the end of the day, comes as a proof of the demonstration of His glory and beauty around us.

In essence, as children of the Kingdom, it is important we understand that God's own type of clothing and covering, and the entirety of the aura around him is not only attractive, it is MAJESTIC in outlook. It goes without saying therefore, that the Lord undoubtedly loves seeing His children looking ATTRACTIVE too! Why do I say so? As mentioned earlier, in some other write-ups I have published, which relates to this discourse, at creation, God intended and still intends we represent him in every way possible on this planet earth, appearance inclusive.

A quick reference to the book of Genesis 1:26, reminds us of the main purpose He created us, which is, to be an extension of His image, an extension of His own unique and peculiar top-notch brand. Halleluiah! Yes! This is why he made us in His image. **"Let us make man in our image, let them be like us in all things….and let them rule their world on our behalf". Yes, we are to look like him in all things, and dressing is not an exception!** *(Genesis 1:26).*

This is so because, aside from his great love for us, he solely created us to be His RESPECTABLE DELEGATES here on

earth, having dominion over other creatures. Friend, the advice therefore is, as much as God grants you the grace, you are expected to be as ATTRACTIVE as you can be, bearing in mind you are a DELEGATE and an Ambassador representing the United Kingdom of Heaven.

Chapter 3
GOD'S FASHION CATALOGUE REVEALED

This chapter chronicles God's experience and profile in the business of dress making, fashion designing and **make up** cum **make over artistry skills**. Basically, our conversation in this chapter will largely hinge on scriptural backing of this claim. Starting from the book of beginnings, humanly speaking, that is, in the world of human beings, we see God reveal himself first as a DRESS MAKER only. Our reference is taken from the book of Genesis 3:21 as quoted in "The Message" translation below:

"..The Lord God made Leather Clothing for Adam and his wife and dressed them.."

Friends, it is important to note that the biblical account, which has to do with the making of the clothes God made for Adam and wife, began and ended in this short statement as recorded in Genesis 3:21. Curiously, one may wish to ask why did God make just a simple dress which is only good enough to cover their bodies? Again, another relevant question that may come to mind is, why did the bible not record that God took much time to really envision what their clothes should look like, as He painstakingly did in Exodus 28?

As the Lord revealed to me, the REASON is simple. In this particular situation, there was no time for any undue funfare. Neither was it time for long process. This was owing to the fact that, although they were putting on their own type of make-shift clothes, which they hurriedly sewed for themselves, the truth was, they were still more or less naked. How did this happen? ADAM AND HIS WIFE CHOSE THE WRONG FABRIC. This fabric was basically made of "Fig Leaves". The point is, owing to the shameful predicament and embarrassment they found themselves, to make clothes, Mr and Mrs Adam HURRIEDLY, GOT HOLD OF WHAT THEY COULD LAY THEIR HANDS ON. THEY CHOSE TO MAKE DO WITH WHAT WAS WITHIN THEIR REACH AT THAT TIME. THIS WAS LEAVES FROM THE PLANTS AND TREES IN THE ENVIRONMENT. Refreshing our memory, about this fact, when the Lord called out to Adam, unlike before, when he used to be confident to see God, rather, this was his response in Genesis 3:10

"When I heard your voice, I was afraid, so I hid because I was naked".

Therefore, in His divine responsiveness, as a good creator, caring father, God needed to do something quick about their matter! While He did not want to leave them in that shameful state because they represented His image on earth, again, while God needed to protect His image and trademark which they were leaving with, (appearance-wise, as they were being prepared to be sent out compulsorily out of the garden of Eden, a place which I term - Garden of Peace, honour, security and abundance of all good things), He (God) could not afford to waste time on secondary matters as, making specially designed clothes for them. The primary matter arising, at that moment was about the purpose, that is the essence for that item of clothing, which was, to cover them up. Friend, this was urgent! It was to shield them away from shame and the much embarrassment they caused and consequently had found themselves.

The following scripture in the book of Genesis lays credence to the seriousness of their naked or semi-naked state. This equally brought about the need to quickly fix the mess, and as far as God was concerned, this was most paramount.

"..Then the man and his wife heard the sound of the Lord walking in the garden, in the cool of the day, and they hid from the Lord, among the trees in the garden. But the Lord God called to the man, saying.."Where are you?"

"And Adam said, "I heard you in the garden, and I was afraid because I was naked, so I hid". *(Genesis 3:10)*.

Secondly, another reason God had to do a quick one, was to shield them as much as possible from the climate and weather conditions which was becoming harsh by the day. And perhaps that was the reason God went for something like a coat of fur to clothe them. This was because, aside the fact that all of a sudden, the glorious covering they were putting on, by way of clothes, disappeared off their bodies. Consequently, they became exposed to harsh weather conditions and prying eyes around. This was another visible consequence and negative occurrence that greeted their acts of rebellion towards God. Consequently, everything in nature began to go wrong and gradually became less Adam-Friendly, if you like less human-friendly.

If you need details of the revelations God gave me on this very point please go check it out the first 3 chapters of my first book titled "**Does God Care About The Way I Dress**". In the book, details of the awesomeness of their first dress, the consequences of its loss, stemming from their acts of ignorance, disobedience and the subtle rebellion against their Maker, is not particularly the focus of this book and this chapter. The information you have in this very paragraph is just like an attempt to scratch the surface. So please kindly avail yourself of a copy of my 1st book for more details of the unique and rare revelations you may require in this very regard. This book stresses the need to be adequately covered, how much God detests seeing nakedness and how to help the family, body of Christ and the society at large.

Long story short, at that very moment, the circumstances under which the Lord God had to operate when it became expedient and compelling to make them a cloth of covering was not a pleasant one at all. It was indeed a sad one for Him. IT WAS NOT A DAY FOR GOD TO REMEMBER AT ALL! He was not happy with them. Therefore, it was not time to give the impression He was out to celebrate their defeat by making them a ceremonial or beautiful garment. Otherwise, this would send wrong signals and could be tantamount to condoning indiscipline of the highest order. They needed just a simple dress to cover their nakedness, shame and human dignity, and the Lord did just that! It was indeed a cloth made under a sobering circumstance, with no funfair needed. So, friend, this was God's first work in dress making. It is expedient to underline that this was in the context of human experience. <u>The point is, where Purpose differs, the Need to create would equally differ as well</u>. And as the saying goes NECESSITY IS THE MOTHER OF INVENTION.

Now, as events in human history vis-a-vis God's interaction and encounter progressed, it is interesting and gladdening to discover how our heavenly Father's disposition gradually evolved and changed for our good. This I must say, was indeed a pleasant one! This was

about how God would have us covered, the best way possible. In this new circumstance, one could say the relationship between God and man had metamorphosed overtime through his grace and mercy, such that, regardless he now allows us assume the responsibility of representing Him here. And this is in accordance to the original purpose he made us, not just as a king but now as situation demands - as a priest. And talking about the idea of "man, playing the role of a priest", it is expedient to note that, then, under the dispensation of the old testament, only few men who were assessed to be fit by character, family lineage wise, or as God deemed fit, were chosen by God to serve Him in such capacity. These ones, were the privilege few called, to carry out this all-important and sensitive role. The role which was like a go-between God and Man Race. The role of a Priest.

Therefore, because they (the priests and ministers alike) were not just representing God among men, they were at the same time representing men before God and in His glorious presence. God takes the office as a special role and a prestigious position to occupy. Consequently, the demands or the ethics of the office calls for a dignifying appearance. And if a man who has dignity is to serve in the place of dignity, then, an appropriate dress, being an expression of the dignity of the office is expedient here.

Little wonder then, why this time around, the good Lord, the God I fondly call the Author of Beauty, Fashion, Life and Style ushers us into a completely new experience which is the second phase in the chronicle of his expertise in the business of dress making. This time, God was seeing expressing his stunning statement in the arts of fashion designing. Please go see for yourself, some relevant quotations from the amazing fashion statement, as vividly spelt out in many scriptures. Key among them is the account in the whole of Exodus 28. As mentioned earlier, it would interest you to discover how stunning, stylish and awesome His own fashion statement could be!

The finesse, precision, intricacies, professionalism, uniqueness and cost of the expensive materials used, goes a long way in giving us a dint of idea about how gorgeous and excellent God's own fashion statement can be. This also goes to show how much premium God places on good looks. A popular saying goes "**Looking good is seriousness business**". With God, we can see here that God takes much more seriously than we think the issue of seeing his children and ministers looking good and great in their dress statements. Check this scripture out: Exodus 28. Here are some excerpts from the chapter laying credence to the fact that God loves beautiful outfits, particularly on his own children:

3)."….Tell all who are experts, whom I have endowed with skill and good judgment, that they shall make Aaron's garments to sanctify him for My priesthood….they shall use fine linen ……and they shall make ephod of gold, blue, purple, and scarlet (stuff), and fine twined linen, skillfully woven and worked……the skillfully woven girding band which is on the ephod shall be made of the same colours of gold, blue, purple and scarlet and fine twined linen……and you shall make sockets or rosettes of gold for settings…….

…..and two chains of pure gold, like cords shall you twist them, and fasten the corded chains to the settings…..the breastplate shall be square and doubled, nine inches in length and nine inches in breadth………

….you shall set in four rows……these precious stones. On the first row arrange…..carnelian, topaz, carbuncle. On the second row put emerald/ruby, sapphire and diamond. On the third row, a jacinth, an agate and an amethyst. And on the fourth row, a beryl, an onyx, and a jasper; they shall be set in gold filigree……all the stones shall be twelve.

……you shall make for the breastplate, chains of pure gold twisted like cords (two in number)….and you shall take the two gold rings and attach them to the lower part of the two shoulder pieces of the ephod in front, close by where they join, above the skillfully woven girdle or band of the ephod…..and they shall bind the breastplate by its rings to the rings of the ephod with a lace of blue, that it may be above the skillfully woven girding band of the ephod, and the breastplate may not become loose from the ephod……

…Make the robe (to be worn beneath) the ephod all of blue….and there shall be a hole in the centre of it (to slip over the head), with a binding of woven (a hem around on the edge) around the hole, like the opening on a garment, that it may not fray or tear….and you shall weave the long and sleeved tunic of checker work of fine linen ….and make a turban of fine linen or silk…..you shall make a girdle, the work of the embroiderer…………..

…..for Aaron's sons, you shall make long and sleeved tunics and belts or sashes and caps, for glory and honour and beauty………..

In the light of the above, we are able to see that no doubt, God is awesome in His own beauty statements. Indeed it is evident that God has a great sense of beauty. For point of emphasis may I reiterate here that, more fascinating is the discovery that he's got a high taste for fashion and style!

God's profile in the expertise of Dress Making and Fashion Designing, which chronicles from making of simple coats as recorded in the book of Genesis 3, to the prowess and dexterity displayed in the exquisite design of a very elegant and flamboyant dress code in Exodus 28, only goes to show that God's interest in fashion is always evolving according and for specific purposes and to His glory at the end. The intricacies which went into the dress He designed was vividly spelt out in the directives He gave, revealing that the rare artistic skills and touch of elegance displayed by Him is second to none!

To crown it all, as if putting icing on the expertise of dress making and fashion designing, such as we have seen so far, further reading into subsequent books in the old testament introduces God again as someone who does not only appreciate good and fanciful clothes but someone who also, can further beautify his own children with appropriate make up and make over touch. Thereby making them look more radiant, appealing, stunning enough to look like Kings, and in this particular instance, Queens. Let us check out a proverbial daughter, better still proverbial bride-to-be of God became unbelievably transformed from a repelling state to a radiant state admirable by all who saw her. This is according to the book of Ezekiel 16:6-14. And the credit? The credit goes to God whose account of His own profile in beauty therapy treatment, made this young lady a cynosure of all eyes, even on a global level, such that she became a renowned queen! Please note that this is a complete different story from Esther's. The queen being described here was even more famous than queen Esther. She was a world class queen more or less. Her beauty and fame surpassed that of Esther, so to speak. This was how God described her after He dressed her up. This is below quoted:

…..when you were born, you were not bathed and cleaned up, you were not rubbed with salt, you were not wrapped in a baby blanket. No one cared for you…in tenderly ways…You were thrown out into a vacant lot and left there, dirty and unwashed…..and then I came by..saw you in a bloody and miserable state, lying helpless and filthy. And I declared my plan and good thoughts towards you – "Live! Grow up like a plant in the field!" And you did. You grew up. You grew tall and matured as woman, full breasted, with flowing hair. But you were naked and vulnerable, fragile and exposed.

"I came by again and saw you, saw that you were ready for love and mature enough to have a lover (husband)…so I took care of you, dressed you and protected you….you became mine. I gave you a good bath, washing off all that old blood, and anointed you with aromatic oils.   I dressed you in a colourful gown and put leather sandals on your feet. I gave you linen blouses and a fashionable wardrobe of expensive clothing (costly fabric)   I adorned you with jewelry: I placed bracelets on your wrists, fitted you out with a necklace, emerald rings, sapphire earrings, (for your nose rings and earrings) and a diamond tiara crown for your head.   You were even provided with everything precious and beautiful, namely exquisite clothes and elegant food, garnished with honey and oil. YOUR LOOK BECAME ABSOLUTELY STUNNING.   YOU WERE A QUEEN! YOU BECAME WORLD-FAMOUS, A LEGENDARY BEAUTY BROUGHT TO PERFECTION BY MY ADORNMENTS……..". *(Ezekiel 16)*

"…The amplified version puts it this way in verse 14: "and your fame spread among the nations on account of your beauty, because the splendor I had given you

made your beauty perfect, declares the Sovereign Lord…"

Concluding on this chapter, the portions of the bible highlighted and discussed are few of the scriptures whereby the God Almighty made us understand that, indeed, He is the creator of beauty together with all lovely fashion and lifestyle. What's more? He equally took time out to model for us how we can partake enjoy and even worship him with them. Why do I say so? The Essence of blessing you and I receive from God is basically for one purpose. It is for us to display His glory here on earth and above all, give Him pleasure there from. How do I know this? The bible says "God created you and I, together with all these beauty and fashion concepts, for us to worship him and above all GIVE HIM PLEASURE! "…*For you God, created all things for your own pleasure*". And the question is, "Friend, taking a Self-Fashion Audit or Stock of your Fashion statements, can you honestly say, you give God pleasure in those clothes you flaunt around? Simply put, is the Lord pleased with the kind of Fashion statements you opt for? Or are you just out to please yourself, your circle of friends, fans, followers on social media or financiers. Which of the Fs do you place most value on? The Father, Friends, Fans or Followers.

Perhaps you are at a loss, as a way forward, you could carefully and prayerfully read through the whole of Ezekiel 16. This way, you will get your mind better illuminated as to what informed God's recounting of how beautifully he dressed the queen who became a world class personality. Thanks to God's make over and beauty touch given to the young lady: (an imagery of some sort), and what He (the beautician) actually expects in return, particularly when He decides to extend same grace to you, to be so dressed up, admirable and beautiful. If I may advise, I seriously encourage every reader of this book, to please make effort to get the whole gist about what informed Ezekiel 16, by simply reading the whole chapter. And may God bless you as you do so.

Chapter 4
BEING ATTRACTIVE, NOT SYNONYMOUS WITH BEING SEDUCTIVE

Having established that the God of the Christian faith loves to see his children looking bright and radiant in every way possible, again, much as looking good and attractive is a welcome idea in Christendom, it has been observed that some Christian individuals both men and ladies alike, particularly our female folk, do not seem to understand what being attractive and being seductive is about. Simply put, in the way they dress, it appears they aren't able to differentiate between what constitutes ATTRACTIVE DRESSING and what SEDUCTIVE DRESSING entails.

Little wonder this people accept to wear any design and style thrown at them to put on or model. The good and admirable thing about this category of the Christian female folk is, they are fashion conscious and so, are fashionable. However, they seem to be ignorant about the need to strike a balance between fashion and decency. As a result, particularly with those of them who are in the Christian faith, in the name of trying to be fashionable at all cost, what they wear more often than not, portrays them as fellows who are suffering from what I call an "IDENTITY CRISIS SYNDROME". This people, though profess to be Christians, fail to express the culture, norms and values of the person and the kingdom they represent. Today, it is an understatement to state that there is a huge deficit in Christian Modesty in Dressing.

Now, before we go on, let us consider what being attractive and what looking seductive is all about. It is instructive to state here that the word Attractive is not in any way Synonymous with the term Seductive. And the reason is simple. Anything that has

ATTRACTIVE features naturally, possess POSITIVE and PLEASANT impact on its audience or anything around it. On the other hand, the SEDUCTIVE objects have a subtle DESTRUCTIVE and UNPLEASANT effects on those who knowingly or unknowingly come in contact with them. In essence, seductive clothes on those who wear them, have ungodly or immoral influence on the emotional psyche of the victims who interact with them or see them, either accidentally or by deliberate viewing.

Throwing more light, the phrase "to Seduce" as defined by Oxford Advanced Learner's dictionary means "*to persuade somebody to do something that they would not usually agree to do by making it seem very 'attractive' and the word seducer/seductress also means, a person or a woman who persuades people to have sex with them.* From the foregoing therefore, the word SEDUCTIVE would be clearly understood already, to mean, a sexually attractive thing or fellow. Or something that seems attractive, but in actual fact, is immorally seductive.

Now, what does the bible say about the act of SEDUCING OTHERS under any guise?. **"Now the Spirit speaketh expressly, than in the latter times some shall depart from the faith, giving heed to SEDUCING SPIRITS, and doctrines of devils..".** *(1Timothy 4:1).*

Please permit me to mention here again that, if you need a deep insight into the scripture above vis-à-vis the point of discourse, please get a copy of my first book titled: "DOES GOD CARE ABOUT THE WAY I DRESS?". It is available on Amazon.

Now at this junction as I conclude with this chapter, the Lord asked me to inform all Christian Fashion Enthusiasts that you can EAT YOUR CAKE AND HAVE IT AT THE SAME TIME IN THE FASHION. This is particularly with regard to the scripture which says: "You are a chosen generation, a **royal priest**hood, a holy nation, a **peculiar** people who has been called out of the kingdom of darkness into the kingdom of light of his dear son". This is found in 1st Peter 9:10.

This scripture makes us to understand that being royal in outlook is about being attractive and impressive and being priestlike in appearance is about being decent, modest, godly or God fearing. It's about being a good example for others to follow or emulate. It is about being a Model in every area of life, even as God has called us to be. Yes you can be attractive, fashionable and still appear godly at the same time. You can please God in your dressing, at the same time have pleasure in what you wear. It is all about having a sense of balance and moderation, such that we do not have to be at either extremes of life. This is the reason, the bible enjoins us to apply moderation brakes in all things, particularly when we are tempted to fully express the freedom at our disposal. We should learn not to go overboard as much as possible. Otherwise, we begin to experience frictions with our spirit and our body.

A WORD FOR FASHION MODELS OF THE CHRISTIAN FAITH

It is instructive to state here that, much as one is free to choose one's career, which I find perfectly okay, our models who wear indecent clothes, in particular those who think they have the fear of God in their hearts, that is, those of the Christian faith (being our focus here), need to begin to re-direct their energy towards a more purposeful venture with Kingdom values, such as could be approved by God. This is because, it is by this they would discover their true place in the fashion world. Thereafter, they would definitely find true fulfillment and enduring gains. And this would be without jeopardizing their place with God. Why do I say so?

Now, talking about Models who would like to improve on their sense of godly judgment regarding our point of discourse, and therefore seem to be at crossroads, the question is, what is the way forward? Please note, most ordinary fashion lovers are equally guilty of this societal fashion menace. These are the category I called Non-Models Fashion Enthusiasts. Sadly, these are more in number. The point is, it is not models alone who wear some weird and seductive clothing items. It's just that the models take drivers' seat in fashion updates, thereby, knowingly or unknowingly guide or misguide others, as the case may be.

The bible says in the book of 2 Timothy 2:15 (NIV) "Do **your best to present yourself to God as one approved, a worker, who does not need to be ashamed and who correctly handles the word of truth**". And paraphrasing, in order to bring the central message of this write-up alive better, this means: "**Do all you can to be a worker before God, approved by him as you rightly interpret and model his word through your dressing as an ordinary fashion lover or as a fashion and beauty model, in such a way as to be a blessing to God, yourself and others in and outside the faith.** This is towards building and nurturing others and not to destroy their moral psyche. It is not also about misleading the younger and upcoming models after you. Otherwise, you would end up in shame at the end before God.'...and in our context we say .."**Study to show yourself a good employee in God's vineyard and a good instrument in the hands of Christ by being a good Christian Model of Fashion and Beauty rightly modeling for fashion enthusiasts.** *2 Timothy 2:15.*

In other words, do not perish out of knowledge, and that is the reason the word of God enjoins us to study the bible well enough to know how God will have us go about our own modeling. Friend, either you are a fashion model or simply a fashion lover and enthusiasts, as a child of God, please note that you were not created for the pleasure of the designer. Rather, you were created to please God first, and then yourself before any other thing. Therefore, do not be a slave to money or to fame, by jettisoning God's own preference in your choice of clothes and general appearance. And talking about, the way forward, you may engage in Modeling Christ through Beauty, Fashion and other means of Good and Godly Pageant Shows of your choice, provided it takes you a step further towards heaven and not the one that takes you seven steps backwards and father from heaven.

As I mentioned earlier, please note it is not only fashion and beauty models who are guilty of this indecent lifestyle. Even non-models and Christian individuals alike fall short of having DECENT WARDROBES. It is more disturbing with this other category of people because they are more in number. As such, are found in every part of the society and nations. Here, we are referring to ordinary fashion lovers, who are in the general category. These are simply passionate and love to wear trendy clothes just for pleasure or as a lifestyle and self satisfaction. Cutting long story short, it is the majority of our Christian population that have this problem. Yes, the majority have the problem which I call the IDENTITY CRISIS SYNDROME. As led by the spirit, it is instructive to state that, God asked me to tell those who wear indecent clothes that, as Christians, they are actually suffering from identity crisis syndrome. In addition, the particular syndrome they are actually suffering from is the Concept God tagged the syndrome in the Tree of Knowledge of Good and Evil". This tree according to the account in

Genesis 3 was located in the middle of the garden of Eden.

And talking about the relationship the first delegates of God on earth, that is, Mr and Mrs Adam, had with this tree (having both good and bad qualities), the point is, the Lord specifically warned and forbade them not to interact with it, much less feed from it. However, they did not get it. So they lost out in the end. The reason is simple. Though, the fruits on the tree appeared same, tempting and appetizing, however it was of DUAL IDENTITY! It was what I call IRRESISTIBLY SEDUCTIVE, and they were not smart enough to recognize this. Friends, this tree of dual identity is quite similar in nature with a typical Trending Dress or Popular style that has both good and bad qualities. As a child of God, in the name of trying to be in tune with what's in vogue and trending, when you choose to wear indecent stuff, this gives you away as a confused believer, or a Christian with an I.D crisis syndrome.

The point is those GOOD and BAD or All In-One DESIGNS are not really good for the special person God called you in 1st Peter 2:9.   Those modern and trendy wears with these bad designs, are actually good in some ways. For instance, because of their durability, beauty, fancy and its uniqueness which make the wearer stand out distinctively in the crowd.   However, the same attires have negative and evil effects on people because of its design and style, which accentuates or exposes sensitive parts of the body in such indiscriminate, inconsiderate, irresponsible and indecent manner.

Whereas, common sense tells us that when something is described as Good and Bad at the same time, it is something DANGEROUS and RISKY to mess around or interact with, it is sad to note that nowadays, many Eves today are seen still going for such Eden fruits of indecent wears.

This is largely typical of clothes which expose your laps (above the knee-level skirts and above the tummy blouses, gowns above the knee-level, trendy clothes revealing your cleavage, tummy or too much of your back, body hugging clothes which accentuates the feminine -private body contours in a nauseating and tempting manner, and the most common, wearing of trousers with blouses that do not sufficiently cover the hips curves (bucks, well enough). Brethren, for me wearing of trousers is not a bad thing in itself, it is how you wear it that matters. Friend, the list is endless. In this regard, my prayer is, may the Lord have mercy on His church. This is because some even dare to wear these immodest trendy wears to church. Some even go as far as mounting the Holy

Altar of God with it and even minister on the altar. As if the altar is just like any other stage, podium or performing place, and no longer the SACRED meeting place of the most high.

Keeping long story short, God's message for all his beautiful daughters and of course sons is: "TO BE ATTRACTIVE, YOU DON'T HAVE TO BE SEDUCTIVE". Being attractive is not in anyway synonymous with being seductive. As a sound, heaven bound and heaven conscious Christian, being attractive is not about being careless, irresponsible, inconsiderate, unreasonable, carefree and unrapturable.

Now, concluding, friend, before you put on any cloth, please remember first, WHO and WHERE you represent. Who you are, is an Image and extension of God Almighty (through the Lord Jesus Christ), and WHERE you represent is the Kingdom of God. How do I know? What makes it clear about who you are and why you were created is embedded in the essence of your creation as recorded in Genesis 1:26. And as to where you represent, the bible says we are foreigners on this earth, our real country home is heaven. So learn to reflect your own heavenly cultural heritage even as you have fun in the fashion world here on earth.

The point is, having fun with fashion is not bad. However having inordinate fun at God's expense or at the expense of making heaven is what is bad. Remember the popular maxim which says, "DRESS THE WAY YOU WANT TO BE ADDRESSED". How you want humans to address you, you may dress that way. And more importantly, the Lord asked me to tell you to learn to: "DRESS THE WAY YOU WANT GOD TO ASSESS YOU AT THE END OF YOUR LIFE'S JOURNEY".

Finally, in the light of the above, we could now conclude that indeed God's fashion statement is attractive and good to behold, discover, experience, savour and emulate. More importantly, it is absolutely safe and sane to model for others and enjoy oneself to the glory of His name and accomplishment of his grand agenda for mankind which is, to eventually bring all back to himself at the end. And this is the essence of God's own fashion, beauty life and style! As I always say, and I repeat here, God does not do anything without a purpose. In essence, what I mean to underscore here is, fashion, beauty and style are all means to an end. And as far as the goal of this write up is concerned, that end is heaven. **So, I pray, may we all end in heaven, using fashion, beauty and style as one of those means to enter rather than means that could deter us from entering. Jesus says "DO ALL YOU CAN TO ENTER THE KINGDOM OF GOD, BECAUSE MANY WOULD STRIVE TO ENTER, BUT WOULD NOT BE ABLE TO". Lastly, RULE OVER FASHION, DO NOT LET FASHION OR BEAUTY RULE**

OVER YOU! Remember you are to have dominion over these things, not the other way round – Genesis 1:26.

Please watch out for my next book which promises to be more exciting, entertaining and spiritually refreshing

God bless you for reading!

References

1. Peculiar Revelations and Inspiration

    From The Holy Spirit

2. The Holy Bible

3. *"Does God Care About the Way I*

    Dress?", by Ope Fodeke-2012

Other Books and Publications by the Author

1. *"Does God Care About the Way I Dress?"* 2012

2. *"Are You a Dressed Chicken….?"*, 2013

3. *"Psalm 23: The Shepherd's Indispensable Business Manual for Today's Business-Driven Christians"*, 2015

4. *"..Beauty Pageant Express Mini-Magazine", A publication of Peculiar Revelations Broadcast 2019*

5. *"Aso Ebi: Your Visa To Heaven! " (Family Dress Code), 2020*

The Book

FASCINATING IS IT to discover that God's got a high taste for fashion and style! More exciting is His great sense of Beauty. God's profile in the expertise of Dress Making and Fashion Designing is aptly revealed in this piece, chronicling making simple clothes, to the dexterity He displayed in the exquisite design of a very elegant and flamboyant dress code. What's more? His fashion statement, moves to a crescendo as a top notch beautician and make-over expert.

Who should read this book? Beauty Enthusiasts, Fashion Lovers, Beauty Experts, Beauticians and Fashion Designers alike. Ministers of God seeking rich and engaging reservoir of knowledge, which could equip them in enlightening Christ's Flock in their care on matters regarding admirable and decent fashion statements in a way to derive maximum benefits for entertainment, effective branding, dominion in the fashion world and the entire world's space.

The Author

Ope Fodeke, the coordinator of ''Peculiar Revelations Broadcast'' holds B.A(Ed) French, from Obafemi Awolowo University and Masters in Public Administration (MPA), LASU. Her approach in revealing God's message is uniquely inspirational, engaging and rare; privileged to speak at Christian Youth Programmes, NYSC Fellowships, Teens' Camps, Christian Women Forums, Single Ladies Meetings and Guest Speaker at School Events. She is An Applauded Author of four books. Her services have been engaged for Writing in Magazines, Newsletters, Editing and Proofreading. She was a Snr. Asst. Registrar with the NFLV, a Federal Inter-University Centre in Lagos, Nigeria, Vice Chairman Tako 1 CDA, Ajara, and Asst. Coordinator, Women Wing of the Badagry Chamber of Commerce, Industry, Mines and Agriculture (BACCIMA).